HOW TO MAKE MONEY ONLINE

Dan Conaghan

About the Author

Dan Conaghan has worked with internet and media companies in Europe, Canada and the United States since 1996. From 1996 to 1997 he was editor of Condé Nast Online, responsible for online titles such as Vogue and GQ and for online projects with UK retailers and content-owners. In 1997, he joined Hollinger Digital and founded BestofBritish.com, an ecommerce site, and the UK search portal UKMax.com. In 1999, he joined NewMedia Investors Ltd, advising internet and new media companies on investment and business development. Latterly he has been a principal at NewMedia Spark plc, a leading early-stage internet and technology investment company. He is now an independent consultant and lives in London.

LAWPACK

© 2001 Law Pack Publishing Limited
76-89 Alscot Road
London SE1 3AW

www.lawpack.co.uk

ISBN 1 902646 76 2

Contents

Introduction

Introduction

Let's start as we mean to go on, by using the internet to help answer the question: 'How do I make money online?' If you put these words into the Google search engine, you get 'about 2,310,000' results, so there's plenty to investigate. Even a cursory surf turns up a plethora of different schemes and possibilities, although a good many are of the 'Amazing Second Income' and 'Earn a Living with No Job' variety. However, it is clearly fertile ground for the curious speculator. After wading through the get-rich-quick '$$$' schemes, there are interesting mentions of 'affiliate marketing', 'home working' and 'ecommerce', not to mention many references to online brokerages, for sharedealing and the like. It is a daunting prospect, but nevertheless, an exciting one.

Welcome to what is assuredly the world's biggest marketplace, information resource, talent pool, customer base and consumer paradise: the internet.

Before rushing headlong into the process of trying to make money on the internet, it's vitally important to give this extraordinary phenomenon some perspective. In 2002, the internet seems as commonplace - and certainly as powerful - a medium as television, radio or print. Yet it is still very new. It is only 11 years since the world wide web was first released by the CERN lab, under the guidance of the now legendary developer Tim Berners-Lee, and moved from being largely the preserve of military and academic communities to being accessible by the likes of you and me.

It was only ten years ago, in 1992, that the term 'surfing the internet' was coined, by Jean Armour Polly, only seven since the first net-related company, Netscape, went public, and a mere three since internet access became available to the Saudi Arabian public. Quantifying the internet is now an industry in its own right. We know, for example, that while in 1992 there were just under a million 'hosts', computer systems with a registered IP address, there are now over 150 million. In mid-1993 there were some 130 web sites registered on the world wide web; in mid-2001, there were no fewer than 31,299,592.

These apparently random milestones serve to illustrate the internet's haphazard, not to say chaotic, development and its explosive growth. Nevertheless, in these 11 years, it has grown faster - and in more directions - than any of its inventors could possibly have imagined. It is, if you like, a child prodigy, approaching its teenage years with ever-increasing strength, rapidity and appetite for more knowledge, more reach, more attention.

For all its relative youth, the internet has already proven itself to be a fully fledged mass medium. Like television or print it is capable of generating large amounts of money from myriad revenue streams. It is, after all, an extremely efficient network and marketplace, a forum in which to do business locally and globally. And besides giving employment to millions of people around the world, the internet also offers businesses a new, and potentially lucrative, outlet for their goods and services.

Let's not forget that although it is patently possible to make money online in 2002 and beyond, it is still against the backdrop of the recent boom and bust cycle which has occurred in the past two and a half years. There was, to paraphrase Alan Greenspan, 'irrational exuberance' on the way up and irrational despondency on the way down. Whatever the causes, the effects are still being felt. It is a truism to say that it will never be possible to seduce the markets with dot.com offerings again. Equally, the corrections which occurred on the way down, savage as they were, caused a huge shakeout in the industry. Nowadays, analysts are much more cautious about the viability of online business models. But they are unanimous about the future of the internet: it is here to stay, it is here to grow, and it is a huge commercial force to be reckoned with.

Business models

The online world is littered with jargon, but some of it is useful to have to hand to distinguish one field of internet business from another. The most important distinctions are now well-established business concepts:

B2B - Business to Business. One of the most common online business models, where businesses interact with one another, creating efficiencies and cost savings along the way. In trading exchanges, for example, large numbers of buyers and sellers meet and transact. Examples are E Steel, Chemdex or PaperExchange, each servicing their respective industry and, more often than not, set up by veterans of those (offline) industries.

B2C - Business to Consumer. Simply, where a business is selling an item to a consumer in a retail environment. Amazon.co.uk, Travelocity.co.uk or Firebox.com are all examples. This was the sector that attracted most new entrants during the recent dot.com boom and had the most casualties during the subsequent bust. But many are still thriving and look set to become mega-brands in the same way as many of our High Street businesses are.

C2B - Consumer to Business. Not so common, but typified by Priceline.com a cool idea embodied in a travel, goods and services web site where customers make offers to, for example, airlines along the lines of 'I'm prepared to pay up to $100 to fly from New York to Boston. Make me an offer'. Essentially, the consumer states the price.

C2C - Consumer to Consumer. eBay, the online auction marketplace is a prime example, where one punter offers for sale an item and another bids for it. A classic use of the internet, this immediately caught people's imagination and remains a favourite cut-out-the-middleman business model. This is sometimes called 'P2P', or Peer to Peer, when the system involves file-sharing. Napster, the online music sharing service is a typical P2P application.

Chapter 1

Selling goods and services online

Chapter 1

Selling goods and services online

Summary

· Introduction
· What sells online and what doesn't
· Winners and losers
· Obstacles to selling online
· Fulfilment and delivery
· Conclusion

Introduction

The first thing to say about selling goods and services online is: learn from others' mistakes as well as their successes. After the 1999-2000 shakeout, it is abundantly clear that a great deal of money was wasted on trying to create businesses that had no hope of success. The old cliché that it's the pioneers who end up with the arrows in their back rings true. The once-mighty Boo's and WebVans of the world, along with a multitude of smaller players, all made a similar contribution to the boom and bust: they taught their successors some very good 'How Not To…' lessons.

Back in the mid-90s, when most large businesses in the UK had embraced the internet only to the extent of posting some 'brochureware' online, there were many sceptics about whether anyone would buy anything online. There were widespread concerns about a huge range of issues, including security, about whether people would buy goods they couldn't pick up and handle and whether web sites would be swamped with returns. They were all valid concerns and some proved to be true, but equally many have been largely disproved as more and more consumers have become comfortable shopping online.

What sells online and what doesn't?

There is no definitive answer, because often success or otherwise depends not so much on what you sell as how you sell it and, indeed, how you manage the business and the brand.

One industry observer, Professor Michael Rappa, has summed up the generic forms of business models on the web as follows, including his examples:

- **Brokerage** - eTrade, Carsdirect, Chemconnect, VerticalNet, Yahoo! Store, eBay, Priceline, Respond.com, Dealtime, MySimon, Bountyquest

- **Advertising** - Excite, Yahoo!, Cybergold, Netcentives, FreeMerchant, BlueMountain

- **Infomediary** - NetZero, ePinions

- **Merchant** - Facetime, Gap, Land's End, Amazon

- **Manufacturer** - Flowerbud, bmwfilms.com

- **Affiliate** - BeFree, i-revenue.net

- **Community** - Deja, ExpertCentral, Abuzz, Guru

- **Subscription** - Wall St Journal, Slate

- **Utility** - FatBrain, Authentica

Although the above may exist in isolation, often an online business will use more than one to execute its strategy. But if you take a few moments to examine some of those web sites chosen by Professor Rappa, you can see where he is drawing distinctions between business models. It may help you to define the arena where you want to play and to segment the market properly. So, from the outset, we can see that there are some fundamental questions which anyone wanting to make money online has to ask themselves, the first of which we can take from the professor:

- Which business model?

- What am I selling?

- What is the audience?

- What is the competition?

Let's assume that the first question is answered by your examination of the above models, and the next question is 'What to sell?' Here, it's worth trying to segment what currently sells online, with varying degrees of success:

- Travel services

- Books, music, entertainment

- Clothes, accessories, fashion items

- Life purchases (cars, homes and mortgages)

- Information services

- Financial services

Everyone who has used the internet for a reasonable length of time will be able to name a site or two which sells the above, whether it's Amazon for books, HMV for music, Jamjar for cars or Expedia for travel. The fact that these are now household names must prove that they're successful, right? Not necessarily. Some of the biggest online brands are loss making, have been since day one and expect to be so for quite a long time yet. In many cases, it's a long, long haul to profitability. A key lesson to learn is how to bridge the funding gap to break-even. Get it wrong by even a few months and even the most promising business can go to the wall, or at least be savaged by the vultures circling overhead.

Nevertheless, it's fair to say that in all the categories above, there are indeed well-funded, profitable or getting-there businesses which have proved that they can build brand and survive in tough markets.

Rather than dwell too long on the mega-brands like Amazon, let's look at a tiny brand, Bodas, which sells women's underwear and babywear online and offline. The question is, do clothes sell on the internet? The answer seems to be 'yes', if the product, pitch and fulfilment are right. After a successful career as a lawyer and as a fund manager in the City, Helena Boas set up her own company, Bodas Ltd, in the summer of 2001. The company sells simple, chic women's underwear and babywear from a shop in central London, via a print mail-order catalogue and from a web site at www.bodas.co.uk. For Bodas, the web site has proved an extremely effective sales tool, contributing over 40 per cent of orders over the first quarter of sales (with the remaining 60 per cent coming from mail order).

While Boas had always seen the business working via multi-channels, the level of online sales significantly exceeded expectations and, as a result, just five months on she commissioned the original designers, London-based webshop HugoBlue, to redesign the web site and build in additional functionality. Boas believes that the success of Bodas online has to do with three key elements of their product and business: firstly, the idea is simple and the product range narrow; secondly, the relatively low order value makes people willing to experiment; and thirdly, the goods are easy to deliver/receive via post.

So if Bodas works, why didn't Boo? Vast screeds have already been written to answer that question, including a book by its founders, but having witnessed its extraordinary rise and fall at reasonably close quarters, by being in London and in the industry at the time of its birth, it seems obvious that it failed to put in place even the most basic controls on its business functions. This, coupled with a poorly defined market and a cavalier attitude to money and investors' funds, spelled doom from the beginning.

What of the audiences online businesses are trying to reach - the third question above? It is no good having a brilliant idea if (a) there is no audience or (b) there is an audience but you can't reach it. Often, entrepreneurs fall in love with their ideas and refuse to acknowledge there might be any flaws in their plans. This is a mistake. A common failing is to imagine there are hundreds of thousands of consumers desperate for your product or service; a common finding is that there are not.

In the past 18 months, it has almost become a mantra that businesses 'failed to find their audience' and closed. It's true, it's not easy. A good example might be Clickmango, an inspired idea to sell vitamins, herbal remedies and all manner of 'wellbeing' clobber online. In the autumn of 1999 it raised several million pounds of venture capital funding in record time. It closed its doors a year or so later basically having failed to find its audience among the British public, who were not, it seems, ready to buy their vitamins online in sufficient numbers. It was difficult to fault Clickmango on its management (ex-AOL, Disney and the like), its financial model or its marketing and the site was a masterpiece of funky, but functional design; but the punters didn't buy it. Ironically enough, the story of the business is now a course module at London Business School as a lesson for aspiring entrepreneurs in how to avoid a similar fate.

Of course, you can do all the market research you like and still not find the audience, but the risks can be mitigated by keeping a cool head. Many businesses fail because they attempt too much, too soon. The winners tend to play a long game and husband their cash resources carefully.

What of the competition? Again, this can be something you prefer to block from your mind, but denying it can be dangerous. It is well worth spending time on analysing your comepetition, not least to spot weaknesses you may be able to exploit, on the know-your-enemy principle. If we look at the once overcrowded sectors of internet business - online property listings, booksellers or gardening web sites, for example - it's clear only a few have survived and those will have learned a great deal from their competitors' failings. So ask yourself not only 'What is the competition?' but also 'How can I improve on what they offer?' and 'What are the biggest threats to my idea and my customer base?' These may sound rather like Day One at Management School ideas, but they are often forgotten in the rush to set up businesses.

Ultimately, internet businesses mirror those in the real world and many do not innovate or reinvent the wheel, so much as try to improve on existing businesses: to do the same thing faster, better, cheaper. We've looked very briefly at some key questions. Of course, there are many others which can help get a business off on the right foot. But it's worth taking a look at some winners and losers to put them into perspective.

Winners and losers

It's a fair bet that most people in the UK have heard of Lastminute.com and a sizeable number will have tried the service or registered for its weekly email updates. It can take some of the credit for encouraging people to buy online, to feel comfortable with making a transaction. And it is one of the great dot.com success stories, not least because it has survived the dot.com crash. Yet Lastminute's success comes not only from the fact that it utilises the internet to sell its air tickets, gifts and even financial products, but also from its ability to maintain its profile and constantly extend and enhance its brand. From the beginning it has had a simple message, eloquently expressed and, in part, cocking a snook at some of the retail dinosaurs.

What makes Lastminute different from a thousand other dot.com businesses? In an interview with American financial web site Twst.com, Brent Hoberman, co-founder of Lastminute, summed up the business's competitive advantages as follows:

'Some of the most important competitive advantages and barriers to entry are our strong brand, the fact that we have over three million subscribers to our weekly email newsletter as well as our strong supplier relationships. We currently have over 9,000 supplier relationships, which means that we have great liquidity in our marketplace. We also have recently launched our new technology platform, which was very difficult and painful to implement. People constantly underestimate how hard it is to launch a good ecommerce web site and to get the underlying technology right and this process has taken us a lot of development.'

Let's take a look at how Lastminute makes money, or indeed loses money! Although the business is heading towards profitability (it expects to be profitable in two of its three core markets in mid-2002), to date, it has made spectacular losses. In November 2001, the company announced a whopping 50 per cent jump in full-year pre-tax losses, to £53.7 million, mainly due to depreciation and amortisation charges. Does this matter? No, according to the company's directors, who point to the fact that it had (at September 2001) £46.6 million of cash on its balance sheet, which will see it through to break-even and beyond. Further, in the full-year to November 2001, the site has seen the value of total transactions rise from £34.2 million to £124.2 million. True, many of the margins are very tight, particularly on products such as air tickets, but it's still not bad going. These figures are generated by some 4.2 million registered users, who are attracted by the cheap, spare inventory from airlines and holiday companies, as well as the desire to do something spontaneous, which has been a core message of the business from the start.

I well remember Brent Hoberman, a former management consultant who had grasped the importance of the internet as a conduit for business very quickly, showing me the business plan for a last-minute travel, gifts and services web site back in the spring of 1998. I listened with interest as he outlined the initial conversations he had had with airlines and hotels. Few people could have predicted this embryonic company's success or its spectacular growth. Certainly not me. I declined Brent's offer, to invest the paltry sum of £650,000 in return for 40 per cent of Lastminute, and have regretted it ever since. Having watched it develop literally from its inception I did eventually take a punt on its shares, when it floated on the London Stock Exchange at the dizzying heights of the dot.com boom in March 2000. The shares, floated with great fanfare by Morgan Stanley and offered at 380p are, at time of writing, a more modest 36p. So my initial punt of £2,000 is currently worth £189, just about enough for a week's self-catering on a Greek island.

Despite the dismal performance of my own modest investment in Lastminute, my admiration for its founders is undiminished. However, I continue to believe what I noted back in the spring of 1998, which is that the 'lastminute-ness' of Lastminute's goods and services is, more often than not, in the mind of the user. Really, the plethora of gifts, days out, holidays and air tickets are all available elsewhere at similar prices. To be fair, it's true that the airline seats and hotel rooms can often be at bargain prices because they are so-called 'distressed inventory', i.e. seats or rooms that the suppliers could not otherwise sell. But the real secret of Lastminute's success is the marketing of the last-minute concept, the spirit of spontenaity and its ability to encourage impulse purchasing - on an admittedly colossal scale. Bravo to Brent and Martha, because they have cornered the market in the concept of last-minute deals. In fact, a last minute deal is simply a normal deal conducted in a hurry! So the real lesson of Lastminute is, I continue to believe: marketing, marketing, marketing.

It seemed like a great idea at the time. Foodoo.com was born out of a dream team, including an ex-McKinsey hotshot, a successful 'content guy' who had run his own TV production company and the backing of a reputable venture capital house which stumped up several hundred thousand pounds in seed capital. Its mission was admirably simple: to link a huge recipe database, populated by Britain's best-known chefs, with food and drinks suppliers, from major supermarkets to small, specialist suppliers. It was, if you like, a soup-to-nuts idea, making the most of the efficiencies which the internet patently supplies to busy, hungry people.

The business, a straightforward limited company which had given a stake of around 30 per cent to the venture capitalists in return for their initial investment, would, it was planned, derive its revenues from a number of sources. Firstly, it would take a slice of each transaction generated by a user. It would also resell its content and perhaps branch out into print publishing and television programmes. There were other opportunities such as banner advertising, premium, subscription-based services and so on, which were planned for phase two. The site launched in the spring of 2000, backed up by some clever guerilla marketing and a lot of free publicity from a Sunday newspaper, which had followed its progress as a startup.

Sadly, despite a great deal of hard work, the founders soon realised that Foodoo.com was set to fail. It was too small, and lacked the investment necessary to follow a time-worn dictum of 'get big fast' in order to survive. Further investment was not forthcoming and, in the meantime, it proved very difficult to persuade supermarkets of the vision whereby users would be pushed to their own online sites by Foodoo's content. Furthermore, there were technical hiccups with the database and wrangles with web site designers which pushed deadlines back and caused production schedules to slip.

Although some of Britain's best-known chefs put their name to the site - and some even discussed investing in the business - Foodoo suffered from having a grand vision without the money - or the clout - to change consumers' and retailers' habits effectively. It's true that many of the best businesses succeed because they are in some way 'disruptive' - they change consumer or customer behaviour and open up new markets - but it is a risky game.

So Foodoo failed. It closed some eight or nine months after opening its doors and its founders went on to new projects, older and wiser. It might have stood a chance had it secured new funding, but ultimately its loyal investors failed to be persuaded that it could crack the market. The bottom line, unfortunately, was that there was no bottom line, or at least one that stood up to commercial scrutiny. Revenues were tiny, costs were high and that was the prognosis for many months to come. Ultimately, the risks outweighed the rewards, for both the investors and the management.

Why does any business fail? Weak management? Flawed business model? Market downturn? These, and variations of them, are common themes in stories of failed businesses. While online businesses assuredly share exposure to these dangers, they also have to brave particular risks which are peculiar to their industry, not least its extreme youth and its voracious appetite for cash.

The trap was summed up by Carlos Grande, writing in the Financial Times in late 2001:

'You can't afford to promote the site. But you can't afford not to if you are ever going to increase traffic and hit sales targets.'

Examples of crash-and-burn dot.coms are legion - indeed there are even Death Watch web sites devoted to them - but even well-funded ones which made it to the wire - the public markets - have often failed. Take a company called Gameplay, for example. This online video games retailer, which was backed by such mighty High Street giants as Dixons, British Telecommunications and British Sky Broadcasting, appointed advisors on insolvency in late 2001, after 18 months as a public company during which time it had a rollercoaster ride.

It is a sorry tale. At its peak, in early 2000, Gameplay had a market capitalisation of £798 million. At its nadir, in late 2001, the stockmarket valued it at just £758,000 and it estimated that its net assets, after liabilities, would be worth a pitiful £90,000. Where once it had scores of employees, by late 2001 it had just two: its chief executive Mark Bernstein and its finance director Ted Bechman. What went wrong? More or less everything. The company had aimed to become the European leader in supplying video games to mobile phones and handheld devices and to do so went on what one newspaper called 'an acquisition spree', buying up other companies in other countries. Gameplay soon realised it was running out of cash and revenues remained tiny. The figures which bear this out make painful reading: for the year to 31 July 2001, there were losses of £197.6 million on sales of £79,000. That's right: £79,000. So clearly something was deeply flawed in the products, sales strategy and market appetite. The company blamed the slowdown in the games market in 2000 and the change in investor sentiment towards companies in its field.

Obstacles to selling online

Unfortunately, it's never been as simple as just 'build and they will come', the idea that a cool ecommerce site will simply attract hundreds of thousands of willing customers naturally. It's a tough business. Marketing web sites is covered elsewhere in this guide, but let's take a look at what happens when you actually do have a customer on the doorstep, as it were.

Way back in 1996, when I first started in the internet business, there was an oft-told anecdote about Thresher, the wine merchant, which was an admirably early entrant into the ecommerce game. But there were teething problems. The story goes that a random employee answered a telephone somewhere at head office one day to be greeted with the question: 'How do I put this bottle in my basket?', to which he replied, 'What bottle?' The customer, struggling with the web site, was an early casualty of the lack of integration between on- and offline operations in many companies in those early days.

Obstacles to selling online are often to do with customer service, but there are other hazards, too. Here is the result of some Forrester research into the subject:

Obstacles retailers face in selling online

Obstacle	Total (%)
Inability to touch & feel goods	40%
Order fulfilment	27%
Online adoption curve	23%
Customer experience	21%
Site security	20%
Customer acquisition	19%
Trust	19%
Profitability	14%
Branding	13%

Source: Forrester Research

The problem of 'abandoned shopping carts' continues to exercise retailers. All of us will have been tempted to buy something from a web site only to become frustrated with the payment process and abandon the transaction. The problem is a serious one, as these research entities have found:

Percentage of Abandoned Shopping Carts, 2001

Research entity	Total (%)
Ernst & Young	78%
Yankee Group	77%
Greenfield Online	67%
Forrester Research	65%
Boston Consulting Group	53%
Zona Research	50%
eMarketer	48%

Source: eMarketer, October 2001

Fulfilment and delivery

The efulfilment market is big business and getting bigger. A 2001 report by IDC reckons the market is set to grow from $244 million today to $3.7 billion by 2003.

The research company's white paper 'The Growing Role for e-Fulfilment Specialists - Delivering in a Wired Marketplace' - states:

'IDC believes that if anything inhibits this growth it will not be the "front-end" (i.e. product mix, pricing, customer access to web sites etc), but the failure to generate customer satisfaction as a result of flawed fulfilment solutions.'

Key points made by the report are:

- The fast growth of internet commerce in western Europe is challenging the traditional delivery models and strategies that have been based upon the B2B bricks-and-mortar world.

- Poor delivery can have a devastating effect on a company's business.

- Fulfilment is far more costly and complex than creating an attractive web site and online traders often underestimate the resources, skills and time required to create first class fulfilment.

Case Study - Crocus.co.uk Ltd.

In the autumn of 1999, brothers Mark and Peter Fane, who had spent several years running a successful landscaping and nursery business in Berkshire, formulated a business plan to set up a web site dedicated to Britain's growing millions of gardening enthusiasts. With the backing of London-based venture capital funds and private investors, they launched Crocus.co.uk in the spring of 2000. The web site now offers several thousand plants and gardening products for sale, delivered throughout the UK by Crocus's own fleet of vans and gardener-drivers, and also provides a valuable reference tool for its users. This fulfilment solution is augmented by the use of commercial couriers used by Crocus on a contract basis. After several months of trading, the company was able to identify where in Britain the bulk of its business was coming from, and tailor its van routes accordingly. With the majority of its plants - many of which are fragile and need to be distributed in specially designed cardboard containers - and gardening products being 'picked and packed' at a central nursery facility in Berkshire, the company now has a series of 'trunk' routes across the country which act as the main distribution points. Their local vans then plug into this network and cover more outlying areas. An added benefit for Crocus of having its own vans and drivers is that they have direct contact with their customers, which encourages repeat business and allows up-purchases of additional goods and services to be disseminated.

www.crocus.co.uk

- Outsourcing logistics and customer service to external specialists is now a logical option for ecommerce businesses that want to move quickly.

- Specialists offering a broad array of fulfilment and customer services are best positioned to dominate the efulfilment marketplace as it is the seamless integration of activities such as order processing and management, transaction processing, stock management, picking and packing, delivery, returns management and customer service that will enable the fastest and most customer-oriented fulfilment process.

Efficient fulfilment is clearly a key competence of any online business, not just for those sending products out of a warehouse, but also for those distributing electronic data or online training modules. This 'last mile' between business and customer is the one which your service will be remembered for - for the right or wrong reasons. It is quite a brave decision to take, as Crocus did, actually to have your own vans and drivers to deliver goods, but at least they have confidence that products will arrive safely and on time. On the other hand, those are considerable overheads to bear. Most ecommerce relies on the existing postal and courier systems, which are generally pretty good although far from 100 per cent efficient, particularly when it comes actually to delivering a parcel to someone's door. Go into any postal sorting office and you will see piles of Amazon boxes, failed deliveries, simply because people give their home address as the delivery address and, of course, are at work when the postman calls. I was told by a former colleague in the United States that this was Amazon's biggest headache but try as it might, it could not convince people to take deliveries in their offices. So, fulfilment can be one of the most complex parts on online business, not least because it can fall down so easily on human error.

Case Study - Firebox.com

Gifts, and in particular gadgets, seem a natural online sell. One of the most high-profile retailers in the UK is Firebox.com, which was the brainchild of Mike Smith and Tom Boardman, who met at Birmingham University. First launched in 1998, Firebox.com now sells a range of about 300 of the latest gadgets, games and boys' toys targeted at 18-30-year-old men. What has Smith learned about the medium and the market? 'There wasn't a great deal of careful analysis behind our decision to launch a company in the gadgets and boys' toys space,' he says. 'It was a simple combination of the fact that Tom and I were both passionate about the products we were going to be selling and also realised that no-one else was doing anything similar. We didn't have the financial resources to open a shop or launch a mail order catalogue so we stumbled onto the internet almost by default.' It has proved to be a smart decision because both the audience and the types of products are extremely well suited to online retail. The typical Firebox customer is a technology savvy male in his mid-20s who is comfortable transacting over the internet. Consequently, a relatively large proportion of the total market was already online when the company launched back in 1998. The business would have grown much more slowly if it had been targeting pensioners or pre-teens. Smith says a lot of the success is due to favourable PR. 'Firebox sells products that are new, exciting and unusual and as a result they attract a great deal of media attention,' he says. 'Journalists are keen to feature our products on TV, in newspapers and within consumer magazines so we get a lot of positive coverage at a fraction of the cost of traditional advertising. This kind of exposure would have been much harder to achieve if we were selling more traditional items.' What about the margins on Firebox products? 'The products are not widely available elsewhere and the lack of competition means there is relatively little price pressure. One of the early myths of online retailing was that products had to be discounted, but the audience we are targeting is not especially price sensitive and puts greater emphasis on other factors such as convenience, brand and exclusivity of products. As a consequence, Firebox has always enjoyed relatively strong gross margins,' says Smith. 'This has been achieved during a period when many online companies were aggressively selling products at negative operating margins to try and capture market share. A strategy that has put paid to the plans of many early online retailers. Many etailers that have struggled over the last few years put too great an emphasis on technology and devoted too little time to the fundamentals of retail.' Smith maintains that etailing is essentially just a highly efficient version of traditional mail order. This is a sector that has been around for decades and fully understands the complex nuances of distance selling. 'Rather than reinventing the wheel we drew upon as much of this accumulated knowledge as possible. We specialise in discovering the latest "hot" products long before other retailers are aware of them.' Many etailers have suffered because the items they are selling are not especially well suited to remote retailing. 'Peddling dog food online isn't the smartest idea because the unit cost is very low in comparison to its weight,' says Smith. ' Diamonds, on the other hand have a great weight to value ratio. Firebox products are generally small and easy to ship with a healthy average transaction value of £45. Furthermore, our return rates are very low (approximately 3 per cent) because customers usually have a good idea about what they are going to receive.'

www.firebox.com

Conclusion

- Keep the aforementioned four questions in mind: Which business model? What am I selling? What is the audience? What is the competition?

- Learn from others' mistakes as well as their successes. Don't have any qualms about pillaging the best aspects of other people's businesses and try to improve on them.

- Fulfilment and delivery solutions should be the starting point for any online ecommerce operation. Remember that it may be easier to collaborate with existing operations than build your own from scratch.

Chapter 2

Security, payment and CRM

Chapter 2

Security, payment and CRM

Summary

· Introduction
· Software solutions
· Ecommerce packages
· Usability
· Knowing the customer
· Conclusion

Giving the consumer the confidence to conduct transactions online is one of the internet industry's biggest headaches. It is also, in its own right, a multi-billion dollar industry. Web site privacy and security, anti-virus software, secure payment solutions and data protection are some of the fastest-growing areas of the internet business.

A glance back at the history books shows that security issues have been around a good many years. On 27 October 1980, ARPANET, the forerunner of the internet, ground to a complete halt after being hit by an accidentally propagated status-message virus; in 1994 Arizona law firm Canter & Siegel became the perpetrator of the first major 'spam' when it sent email advertising green card lottery services; hackers started hacking in earnest the following year, with attacks on the CIA, the US Air Force, Britain's Labour Party and NASA; on 17 July 1997 human error was responsible for corrupting millions of .com and .net domains, while the 'I Love You' virus competed with attacks on Yahoo!, Amazon and eBay for front-page newspaper headlines in 2000.

What all these examples show is that security is a major part of online businesses and a major help or hindrance to making money online. When a forged web page made to look like a Bloomberg financial news story raised shares of a fledgling technology company by 31 per cent in April 1999, you can be sure that there were hasty reviews of security at every brokerage and news organisation in town.

Web sites contain valuable information and need protecting from hackers, fraudsters and random visits by viruses (the 2000 Love Bug, for example, which Reuters estimates cost businesses an estimated $8.7bn in lost productivity and clean-up costs). It is a false economy to ignore these silent threats to your business, and vital to make room in your budgets for reputable advice and security products to safeguard your own and customer data, transaction systems and server integrity.

There is still a huge amount of complacency about security. In November 2001, when consulting giant KPMG polled executives in 12 countries, including the UK, it found that 79 per cent of senior management executives wrongly believe that the biggest threat to their ecommerce system security is external. Although most of the respondents thought hackers, poor implementation of security policies and lack of employee awareness were the greatest threats to their systems, in reality, disgruntled or former employees, or external service providers who have a long-term relationship with the company, are most likely to commit an attack, or cause a security breach. The survey also found that: 'Nine per cent of those polled have had a security breach in the past year, and only 17 per cent of those pursued legal action. Fewer than 35 per cent perform security audits on their ecommerce systems, and only half have incident response procedures in place.'

With this in mind, a good starting point for security strategy is an industry body such as the Internet Security Forum, which is based in Cambridge and runs a series of educational conferences in the UK, which are free to attend. Thankfully, there is no hard sell. The forum states: 'Each event focuses on a key topical issue, with the speakers contributions being tailored to suit, so building a complete discussion of the theme within the day. Presentations are neither over technical or too sales orientated - we aim to provide information and answers to problems only.'

What do the forum's conferences cover? Typically, a number of UK security companies, such as RSA, CheckPoint Software and Secure Networks send experts along to discuss topics such as the following: User Authentication and PKI Solutions, Anti-Virus Protection, Outsourcing Solutions and Security for the Smaller

Organisation. There are panel discussions and an opportunity to meet other delegates. If you can't attend in person, the forum will send you the proceedings of the conference by post afterwards.

Software solutions

Needless to say, there is a bewildering array of security software on the market, much of it developed in the United States. Luckily, increased competitiveness has driven prices down over the past few years and there are more packages tailored for small businesses. One leading supplier is Checkpoint, which operates worldwide. Its site at checkpoint.com has a useful resource of white papers and brochures (free, but you have to register your company details - a smart way of gathering potential customer leads) and a range of packaged software solutions for VPNs (virtual private networks, i.e. a private network configured within a public one), which are the most common small-business set-ups.

Although jargon is rife in internet security and, like most jargon, unnecessary, you will keep hearing about public keys and public key infrastructure, or PKI. Checkpoint provides admirably concise definitions:

Public key

The published part of an asymmetric encryption scheme. Public keys are not private information and are included in digital certificates. Public keys can be used for two purposes:

- A sender of a message can use the receiver's public key to encrypt the message. Only the receiver, who holds the private key, can decrypt the message.

- A sender can 'sign' a message or message digest with his or her private key. The receiver uses the sender's public key to determine the authenticity of the message.

Public Key Infrastructure (PKI)

A system of digital signatures, Certificate Authorities and other registration authorities that authenticate the validity of each person involved in a secure transaction. A PKI enables organisations to set up and define the scope and participants of a VPN deployment by establishing a trust relationship between their respective Certificate Authorities. Each certificate authority is then responsible for validating the users of its organization for participation within the VPN.

Source: Checkpoint.com

Because these are now industry standards, you'll come up against them pretty soon during any discussions about internet security, as they are integral to the safeguarding of data and customer information, not least in payment systems for ecommerce.

Security doesn't have to be complicated. Although computer viruses can be dangerous, anti-virus software from companies such as Norton and McAfee are cheap and simple to install. Equally, your network can be protected from so-called 'untrusted' networks (simply ones other than your own, such as the internet itself) by firewalls, which are security gateways. Firewalls are essentially there to track and control communications. They are designed to decide whether to authorise, reject, encrypt or log communications from one node of the network to another. They can also be used to secure sensitive portions of the local network, so you can have concentric rings of security. Again, installing firewalls is relatively straightforward and need not be expensive.

Ecommerce packages

Ecommerce packages come in all shapes and sizes, tailored to small businesses, enterprise level concerns and to suit various business models. There are instant-auction packages and a multiplicity of off-the-shelf B2B software. The first and most popular software has been the pure-play Business to Consumer type which enables small companies to build online shops. Nowadays, many thousands of small businesses in the UK are online to a greater or lesser extent and many have extended their bricks-and-mortar retail operations onto the internet. Typically they have used ecommerce packages which are of relatively simple construction: at their heart is a database of products, which can be populated and altered online to suit available stock levels. The database plugs into a front end, the design of which is template-based, to allow simple construction. Finally, a payment engine linked to the main clearing bank network to allow authorisation and debiting of credit and debit cards completes the picture.

Choosing the right package for your business can be a bewildering experience. Most people take the products recommended by their web site designers, who often act as reseller-partners to large software companies such as Intershop. This company, which launched a popular instant-build product called Intershop 3 in early 1998 has now stepped back to sit higher up the food chain and offer more sophisticated platforms on an ASP basis. The following diagram shows how their model works:

INTERSHOP4

Intershop 4 is the most widely deployed hosting product line enabling Service Providers, such as an ASP, an ISP or a Telco, to offer e-commerce sites for small and medium enterprises. As illustrated below, Service Providers use Intershop 4 to offer hosted e-commerce functionality to multiple small and mid-sized Sellers.

Intershop 4 offers best-in-class hosting and e-commerce functionality allowing you to sell anywhere. The Intershop 4 product line includes ePages, Hosting and Merchant. Together, they provide a logical upgrade path from an entry-level site to and advanced, customizable hosting solution. Each of these solutions come on standard platforms, allowing for quick-deployment, low operating costs, and significant return-on-investment.

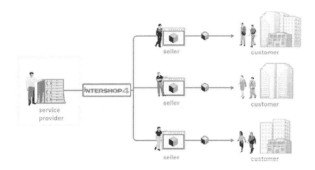

The Intershop model works well for small business people because they are buying into a managed service, which is less likely to go wrong. Increasingly, therefore, the trend is away from having your ecommerce site hosted by a local webshop and more towards a managed service which may look after many hundreds of similar, small web sites.

The first port of call for most businesses looking for an internet and ecommerce presence will be a recommended web design house. There has been a huge shakeout in this sector following the downturn, but the strongest have survived intact. The best yardstick to measure a webshop by is its other clients, so take a close look at their work for other businesses and, if possible, talk to those businesses before committing to a project.

In the past, UK businesses have wasted vast amounts of money on substandard work from ropey design houses with dubious technical knowhow to back up their creative work. Remember, it is very easy to change the look and feel of a web site - really just graphics and 'tables' which control the layout of individual pages - but very difficult to switch database architectures or payment systems. Your ecommerce operation will, ultimately, live or die on its technical platform and not on its colourscheme. So, it's important not to be seduced by funky, creative ideas at the expense of solid technical skills.

Although I certainly wouldn't claim always to have got it right, I've built perhaps a dozen content and ecommerce sites with web designers and technical teams. By about web site number five, I had learned some painful lessons about style and substance. Eventually I settled on a very simple system. Firstly, I would get a technical house, preferably with as few design or creative skills as possible, to build a skeleton site - the database, links, payment and shopping basket plug-ins etc - and deliver it in pure HTML, that is looking like a stripped-down Yahoo! with no colour schemes, photographs, graphics, Java or - God forbid - Flash animations - in place. Then I would sit down and play with the site and ask myself: Does it work? Is it easy to nagivate around? Can I put a product in this shopping basket? And so on. Only when I was satisfied with this basic skeleton would I call in a designer. Even then, their brief would be very simple: a colour palette, minimal graphics and certainly no dodgy animations or stuff which required the user to download plug-ins. Although many of these many now seem simple and obvious precepts, it's still amazing to see clearly expensive web sites being launched today which are badly put together and which, for example, throw a massive Flash animation at the user on their home page. The golden rules remain: keep it simple; test your site on real people before you launch it, and always look for improvements to the navigation or 'customer path' as you go along.

Usability

Whichever ecommerce package you choose, there are still some fundamental issues which rely on human judgment and creative input. One of them is usability - crucial to the success or failure of all online businesses.

Making a web site user-friendly is still a challenge for online businesses, whether they are a High Street giant like Boots or Argos or a small retailer selling country crafts. There is now a growing industry in 'usability' studies, mostly aimed at those High Street giants, which brings focus groups together to study different page-layouts, colours and the ease of navigation. Most of it boils down to common sense. A misplaced 'buy' button or a tortuous shopping basket process will inevitably lead to customer frustration and a lost sale. But some usability issues require more thought and they include innovations which really bring customers back again and again.

Some of these issues were highlighted in a 2001 report by the Henley Centre, commissioned by Touch Clarity Ltd (see case study below). Among other things, it found that online shoppers are still at the very beginning of their learning curve:

'The confusion [during online shopping] is not helped by the fact that even the most experienced internet shoppers have only bought around 20 goods online, giving them the equivalent shopping age of a seven-year-old. Many shoppers struggle to find the online store they want because they can't guess its address or still don't understand how internet addressing works. Even when they find a site they like, many end up there by chance, with little idea how to get back again to make another purchase. To many consumers the name of the internet shop where they bought something is irrelevant, particularly if it is not an existing high street brand. Much like a seven-year-old, they are more concerned with the fact that they have bought something at all, labelling it as "bought on the internet." On another level, online shoppers tend to flock to recognised high street names because it makes them feel safer.' Source: Retail Automation, April 2001.

Usability and customer loyalty go hand-in-hand. Some of the success enjoyed by a retailer such as Amazon is due to its simple design and easy navigation but one of its cutest features remains One Click Ordering, which simply does away with the task of re-entering name, address and credit card details. The module essentially 'recognises' a customer who has registered and made a purchase before and allows them to hasten their transaction.

Once an online business begins to 'recognise' loyal customers it can both reward them and begin to understand the customer activity which shapes the bottom line of the business. This is where usability crosses into the territory known as Customer Relationship Management, a well-established concept which is now at the heart of the world's most successful ecommerce operations.

Knowing the customer

Who is your customer? What do they like and dislike? How often do they visit your web site? When ecommerce first became a reality - and there were widely held views that people would not buy online as late as 1996 in the UK - the answers to all these questions was simply: we don't know. Since the mid-90s, however, the worlds of mathematics and statistics have caught up with the world of retailing and particularly online retailing, whose database-driven model lends itself particularly well to data analysis.

Customer Relationship Management, or CRM, is all about improving a web site's yield, encouraging more spend and more frequent visits. At its most primitive level this might include email marketing of special offers, or asking customers to register valuable data such as their postcode before they buy. At a more sophisticated level, CRM uses mathematical models to determine customers' proclivity to buy product X, based on either their own behaviour, or that of their fellow customers. Once this sort of 'tree of favourites' has been established, it learns.

This intelligent behaviour-gathering technology has been around for some time in the form of 'cookies'. These sit on a web site and extract from your browser some basic information such as the IP address of your computer, the time of your visit and so on. They are controversial, because to some extent they invade customers' privacy. Without entering the whole debate about privacy here, suffice it to say that cookies are largely disliked and have been replaced by less instrusive technology to a large extent.

Just as there is a multitude of different ecommerce packages, there are many CRM solutions which plug into them. Many of these, until recently, have been cumbersome and very expensive - easily running into tens of thousands of pounds. The leading players in this market have been the likes of SAP and Broadvision, which enjoyed huge growth in the mid-90s as ecommerce took off and major corporations such as Ford embraced online business. In the last couple of years, however, mini-versions of these industrial-strength software packages have been designed and many companies have sprung up to compete in the lucrative SME (small and medium enterprises) market. So price points are now a few thousand pounds. And, just as we'll see in the chapter on advertising models, many are offered on a pay-for-performance basis, in which the fee is generated by the gain made by a company utilising the software.

Increasingly, ecommerce companies are realising this makes commercial sense; indeed it is becoming a necessity as the number of online customers grows and their expectations of the service they receive at an ecommerce site increases. The future of eCRM looks bright as more and more people become comfortable buying online and, indeed, are happy releasing their details to providers of goods and services. Although many people are still wary of allowing a retailer too close, others see the benefits of letting them get to know preferences and therefore providing a more tailored service.

Case Study - Touch Clarity

Paul Phillips and Alex Kelleher brought backgrounds in offline customer relationship management and web design respectively to bear on their eCRM business, Touch Clarity. Based in London and established in 2000, the company conducts usability studies for leading ecommerce sites and creates sophisticated software to manage customers and predict their purchasing behaviour. The company's mission is simple: 'Advanced modelling techniques predict and deliver the most relevant content for each customer. Relevant content means they are more likely to stay for longer; to return; and in the case of ecommerce, to purchase - thereby increasing revenue and profit to the site.' The company's Intelligent Personalisation software, which it sells on a licence and ongoing annuity model, observes web site interactions and uses this data to predict future visitor behaviour. The software actually alters content within a web site to maximise business goals. Touch Clarity identifies these as: increased click-through; reduced friction in the purchase cycle; increased customer satisfaction and loyalty, and greater revenues and profits. The company conducted early tests of its software on a greetings cards ecommerce site, sharpcards.com, and was able to present cards to customers which they were mathematically more likely to purchase, based on their online behaviour. This clearly led to greater sales and profitability for the greetings card business, as well as allowing it to carry only relevant inventory. The efficiencies created in the customer purchasing decision therefore could feed all the way back through to inventory management and the design of the web site. www.touchclarity.com.

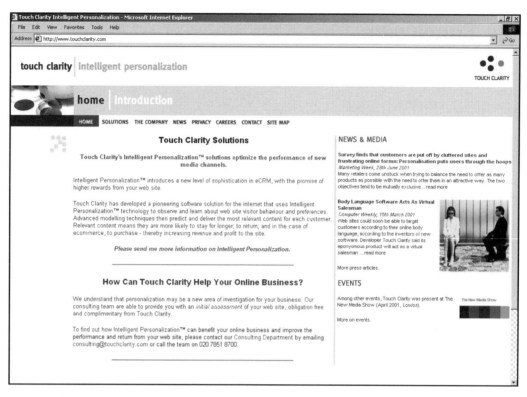

www.touchclarity.com

Conclusion

- Don't economise on security, but take independent advice before buying software.

- Your business begins and ends with the customer. Put yourself in the customer's position when you need some perspective on how to present your online business.

- Online businesses are particularly sensitive to customer behaviour, but are also very well suited to tracking and analysing that behaviour.

- The amount each customer spends, the cost of acquiring a customer and customer 'churn' (how many you can expect to lose and at what rate) are key metrics when external parties come to valuing your business.

Chapter 3

Procurement online

Chapter 3

Procurement online

Summary

· Online trading exchanges
· Staff recruitment online
· Virtual training services
· Conclusion

The internet is well established as a conduit for business efficiencies. It speeds up information flow, connects buyer with seller, enables transactions and much more. Once outlandish ideas, such as allowing one person to track online a parcel on its journey across the world by courier, or connect a job-seeker to a database of carefully targeted employers, are now commonplace. The down-and-dirty businesses which rely on supply chains, procurement and delivery systems are all benefiting hugely from moving key tasks online - and many companies make money in the process.

How does a major industry such as the steel industry move online and make money for its participants? Here is the mission statement for the e-STEEL Exchange, which was launched in 1999 by what is now NewView Technologies Inc:

'e-STEEL Exchange is the leading global marketplace for steel. The exchange enables buyers and sellers of Prime and Non-Prime Products to negotiate, transact, and conclude business with increased efficiency, fewer errors, and reduced cost. e-STEEL Exchange enables users to:

• conduct online, negotiation-based transactions in a neutral, secure environment;

- quickly and accurately target which buyers or sellers should receive a product inquiry or quote;

- make informed and profitable procurement decisions;

- accelerate transaction speed and reduce transaction-related costs across the supply network;

- enhance trading relationships.'

This sums up the advantages of the e-STEEL Exchange, but what about some of the nuts and bolts of the business model? The exchange does not charge the buyer, nor are there any membership or application fees to join the service. Instead, the exchange simply takes a 0.875 per cent cut of the value of the transaction. It calls itself a 'true market' and like other true markets, the e-STEEL Exchange is neutral, does not own any of the products transacted on the system, and is not affiliated with any industry participant.

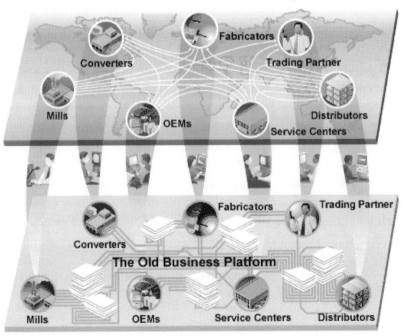

Here's how the company describes the way e-STEEL Exchange works:

'The current way of trading Steel products is plagued with inefficiencies and paper-intensive processes. The e-STEEL Exchange brings the trading process to a higher plane where existing and new relationships are supported while increasing the efficiency and speed of your business transactions. The e-STEEL Exchange, the global online marketplace for steel, is the NEW way of trading steel products, now and for the future. Buyers and Sellers of Prime and Non-Prime Products can negotiate and transact through the secure e-STEEL Exchange. The e-STEEL Exchange enables members to conclude business with increased efficiency, fewer errors and reduced cost.'

Survival

Will B2B exchanges survive? Some will, according to analysts. The business journal eWeek reckons that the survivors will share the fact that they have 'staked out' industries dominated by commodity products and large numbers of highly-fragmented buyers and sellers:

'Consider the chemicals industry. Two independents, ChemConnect and CheMatch.com Inc., have made headway in the trading of commodity chemicals. In fact, since ChemConnect merged with Envera LLC, just one major industry consortium, Elemica Ltd., remains.'

eWeek also identifies another common characteristic of successful independent e-marketplaces:

'They've been astute about conforming to the prevailing business practices in their industry rather than attempting to force more-radical changes than necessary on enterprises that may already be uncomfortable with e-commerce. Altra and Arbinet, for example, allow buyers and sellers to remain anonymous through much of a transaction, a common practice in energy and bandwidth commodity trading.

Independent e-marketplaces must contend with the concern felt by many enterprises that, by using a public exchange, they could risk disrupting relationships with valued business partners and threaten the business advantages that they believe are inherent in their existing business processes, experts say. That's one reason many have begun to embrace private exchanges. With a private exchange, they can model online trading to match their own business processes and avoid the price pressure that using public e-marketplaces could bring.'

So, although there has clearly been a massive shakeout in B2B exchanges, it's clear that the clever and well-funded businesses stand a good chance of carrying on their successful realignment of their respective industries. But some observers are sanguine about the new opportunities afforded by B2B. Accenture, the consulting firm, noted in a recent report:

'The key to success in the B2B online market is not a new business model; rather, it is old-fashioned marketing. We mean the lost discipline of marketing - asking customers what they want and then providing it at a profit.'

Staff recruitment

One of the most explosive areas of online business growth has been in the procurement of companies' greatest asset: their staff. Online recruitment is now a widely accepted business practice and one that clearly creates efficiencies in a notoriously chaotic and paper-intensive field.

For a peek into a simple, but effective, tool for online recruitment, imagine that you want to become an investment banker with Goldman Sachs. On their web site at www.goldmansachs.com the company encourages potential candidates to take an interactive 'personality test'. The questions include 'Which do you prefer? Mechanical toys? or Imaginary toys?' and the like. Depending on your response, you are directed to an area of the bank's business to which you might be suited. I quickly found myself in the dizzying worlds of Corporate Bond Syndicates and Private Wealth Management, which is difficult to extrapolate from my preference for mechanical toys, but we'll let that pass. It's a very simple example of online staff recruitment tools (some of which are very much more sophisticated) and shows how one business filters applicants.

While Goldman Sachs continues to harvest applications directly via its own corporate web site, there is a plethora of online recruitment services which are aimed at the more general jobhunter. One such site, Justpeople.com boasts a weighty database of employers and candidates. It sums up its mission as follows:

'In an online market swamped with "job boards", Justpeople enables employers and candidates to find each other without the need for adverts. Nor does an employer need to trawl through a raft of CVs to find suitable interviewees. The system works through a unique search facility that matches an employer's criteria with the candidate's qualifications and experience. When an employer headhunts using Justpeople, they only find the candidates who meet their demands exactly. When a candidate registers their details, they are only offered jobs that are relevant and of interest to them.'

This concisely sums up some of the advantages of such an online service and it is very much part of a trend. Few Human Resource departments in major companies can afford to ignore online services; equally, many old-fashioned, offline recruitment companies have embraced the internet. In the latter case, this has often led to a collision of cultures and many are now re-examining their online strategies with a more level-headed approach.

So has the internet made recruiting easier? It's a question addressed in a recent poll of 400 respondents, a mix of organizations including: private and public companies, staffing firms, recruiting agencies, non-profit organizations and government agencies. The results were as follows:

Easier - 79 per cent (316 respondents)

Harder - 10 per cent (40 respondents)

Same - 11 per cent (44 respondents)

RecruitersNetwork, which carried out the poll, found that almost 80 per cent of those polled asserted that the internet has simplified the recruiting process. Career sites are easy to use and eliminate the age-old headache of the newspaper classifieds...faxing and approving ads and handling misprints.

The internet also speeds up the recruiting and hiring process. Résumé databases are an instant source of candidates. Job postings are real time, eliminating the wait for the Sunday Classifieds to advertise positions. Résumés are now sent in the form of emails, which are much cleaner and easier to manage than faxed applications.

RecruitersNetwork summed up its poll as follows: '10 per cent of those polled found the internet made the recruiting process more difficult. With any new technology there is a learning curve. Many companies jumped into internet recruiting without a hiring plan, proper training and metrics in place.'

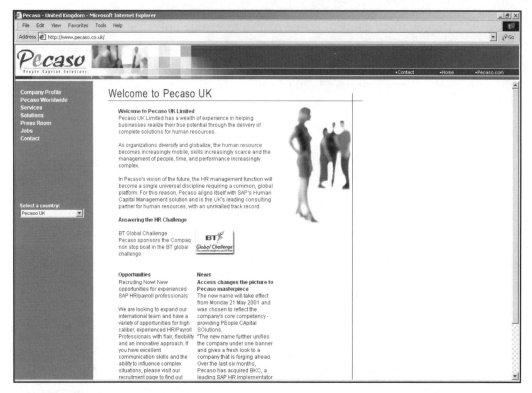

www.pecaso.co.uk

Virtual training

One of the biggest trends in online procurement in recent years has been the explosive growth of online training. To some extent this forms a natural subset of online recruitment, in that once you have a customer who is using your online jobsearch service, why not sell them some online training to go with their new job?

Online training ranges from the simplest Word or Excel courses to highly sophisticated and tailored packages for derivatives traders in City institutions. The fundamental principles of the best online services remain the same: flexibility, self-study and a recourse to professional advice if the student becomes stuck.

Case Study - Pecaso

Pecaso, PEople CApital SOlutions, provides specialised strategic consulting, implementation and support services for IT-based HR solutions and leads the market with new eHR technologies. Through strategic alliances, Pecaso also integrates 'best of breed' applications with existing HR solutions. It has developed many of its own solutions that can be tailored to the requirements of individual organisations, and leverage the investment organisations have made in their ERP solutions. Pecaso addresses erecruitment by providing web-based applications that enrich the core SAP Recruitment functionality. They believe that best practice means integrating external and internal recruitment, blending traditional and web-based channels, and creating an efficient service chain, linking the participants in the recruitment process seamlessly. Pecaso is well positioned to help organisations exploit the benefits of the internet in a way that integrates with their core business systems, providing secure, stable and flexible solutions capable of supporting the most complex of recruitment needs.

Case Study - Beginners.co.uk

Based in Middlesbrough, this online service sums up its business as follows: 'Hundreds of professional online IT and Softskills training courses available for a variety of disciplines and skill levels. Members benefit from a new dimension in spreading the effectiveness of education and training budgets.' For an annual fee of £75, an individual can have access to some 330 online tutorials and 340 training courses and study what they choose at their own pace, along with thousands of daily updated IT jobs and an online email system. Courses are professionally developed by proprietary vendors with strict quality assurance guidelines. The courses range from web development to UNIX skills, Microsoft SQL database construction to advanced computer graphics. The brainchild of two IT professionals, Richard Bendelow and Dean Benson, the site launched with a free service called 'Freeskills' in late 1997 and has since grown with a series of strategic alliances with course providers and other partners. Like many similar companies, it now also sells the software - a 'content syndication engine' - it uses for its own site to third parties. Its core business remains modular courses, easily downloaded by users in Acrobat packages. The company, like many in this sector, has had its ups and downs. Bendelow recently said: 'Since the collapse of internet advertising spends, we have had to reinvent the business model in order make it sustainable, but we have kept true to our original concept of free information. Although we now have membership fees for courses, we have worked hard to keep them modest - over 250 courses for one single membership fee. Consumer and corporate take-up since the launch of Beginners.co.uk shows that we have got the formula right.'

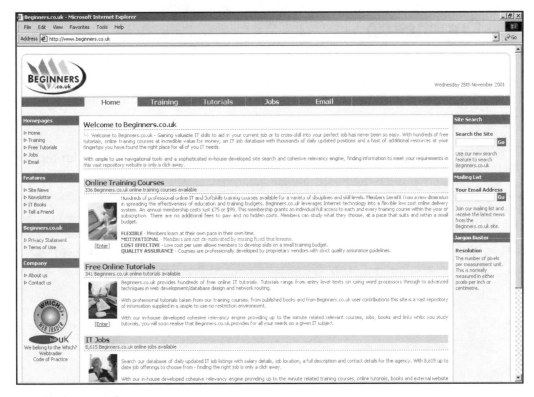

www.beginners.co.uk

Conclusion

- The B2B model is a proven one, but no less susceptible to the downturn than B2C. A trading exchange, for example, is dependent on industry partners and customers just as much as an online bookshop is.

- There are clear efficiencies in moving business services online, but they take time to filter through to real people who are accustomed to offline procedures. It's a long game and you can't change an industry overnight.

- If you are a business customer of an online service, you should expect cost savings to be real and to be passed on to you by the service provider.

Chapter 4

Advertising

Chapter 4

Advertising

Summary

· Introduction
· The UK market
· The future
· Conclusion

Introduction

You need to understand advertising models on the internet if you are (a) intending to advertise your own products online; (b) set up business in the advertising services industries which the medium has spawned; and (c) if you are intending to sell advertising space on a web site.

At first, the advertising arena can seem a daunting area of the internet world, riddled with jargon and, until recently, pretty chaotic with no real rules or accountability, although that is gradually changing. But it is, nevertheless, the lifeblood of the medium and if you've ever clicked on a banner ad and ended up buying a subscription, a book or opening a share trading account you'll understand why: the internet is a battlefield in which brands are built and demolished. And online advertising, which now encompasses not only straightforward 'click me' banner ads but such exotic derivatives as 'interstitials', cookie-driven pop-ups and much more, is key to that process.

It took a surprising amount of time before someone twigged that the internet, specifically consumer-oriented web sites, might be suited to selling advertising. The first banner ads did not appear until October 1994, on hotwired.com, the online presence of Wired magazine and now part of the Terra Lycos network. Those first ads, incidentally, were for Zima (a drink) and for AT&T, the telecommunications giant. People must have 'clicked through', as since those pioneering days, there is barely a well-known brand which has not advertised itself online. And, in under a decade, an entire multi-billion dollar industry in online advertising has sprung up.

Despite the obvious success of some online campaigns and the substantial sums still being spent on them, online advertising is still deemed a long-term player by internet industry observers. Although it has grown extremely rapidly, it has not replaced television, radio or print advertising as the method-of-choice for brand-owners to reach their public. It is still, relatively speaking, in its infancy and some of the fears that it would cannibalise newspaper advertising, for example, have proved unfounded. What online advertising does offer, however, is targeting - and it is uniquely placed to refine that targeting in the coming years.

Like many other areas of the internet, advertising has had its boom and bust cycle. But industry observers say it is anything but dead. In fact, the shakeout has been a huge help. It is undeniably big business. In 2000, US advertisers alone spent $8.2 billion online, compared to $1.8 billion for outdoor advertising and $11.2 billion for the long-established cable-TV advertising market. But it is also worth bearing in mind, as the investment bank Morgan Stanley has pointed out, that the top six US advertisers still spend a mere 1 per cent of the budgets on the web.

In the UK, the patterns are much the same. As the medium matures, the online advertising market - and the metrics by which it is measured - becomes more sophisticated. In the wake of the shakeout and in the current economic downturn, it remains a buyers' market, however. To make money in this game is tough. Where once premium web sites such as financial portals could easily command up to £40 per thousand advertising impressions (counted as each fully downloaded advertising banner), those rates have been halved, or more. Inventories - the amount of space available on a given web site - are half-empty, and those online companies which relied solely on advertising revenues - and they were legion - have long since had to realign their business models or face closure.

As online advertising grows up in this way, it is also becoming more respectable. In 2000, Morgan Stanley reported that online banner ads were more successful at generating brand recall than either TV or newspaper ads. Browsers showed a 27 per cent greater ability to recall a brand after seeing an online ad than before; compare this to magazines at 26 per cent, newspapers at 23 per cent and TV at 17 per cent and you begin to recognise the fact that the internet is a serious force in advertising and marketing techniques.

Equally, advertisers are also looking for a way out of that increasingly outmoded CPM (cost-per-thousand impressions, using the Roman 'M' for thousand) and click-through metrics to measure success. Instead, they are turning to more tried-and-trusted measurements, including brand awareness and likelihood-to-purchase. This is called 'performance pricing' and it is forcing web site owners to prove to advertisers that there is real substance to their traffic figures and oft-quoted user profiles.

This would sound like another variation-on-a-theme dreamt up by some anxious online advertising houses, if it didn't have some blue-chip followers. In the UK, the likes of Dell, Dixons, Mothercare, Argos and Littlewoods have all signed up to pay-for-performance ad networks run by companies such as Commission Junction (CJ) and Tradedoubler. Their idea is a simple one: publishers and advertisers sign up; advertisers choose which sites they want to appear on, while Tradedoubler or CJ sit in the middle, tracking sales and managing payments. Typically, Tradedoubler will charge a set-up fee of £2,900 (CJ is a more modest £885) and both charge 30 per cent of the commission paid by the advertiser. CJ UK claims a chunky 2m sales transactions totaling £68.4 million in the period Jan-Sept 2001. Crucial to the continued success of this 'sell' is the fact that the holy-grail 'click-through' rate (ie the rate at which an online user clicks the banner ad) is 1.9 per cent - about seven times the industry norm. And some 3 per cent of those who click through end up buying something - or at least registering - on the target site. Some practical examples: Virgin pays 75p for each email address it captures using the system, Argos pays 2 per cent on every sale and credit card company Capital One up to £5 per new application.

What this all points to, is that on the internet, the middleman's position is still a good place to be. All those 75p's add up. Taking a piece of the transaction on the way through, as it were, has always been an attractive business model, and the internet is a fruitful place to explore it.

Pay-for-performance is upsetting some of the 'traditional' cost-per-thousand ad sales people, such as AOL, who argue that pay-for-performance ignores the ability to build brands and shape customer behaviour. But in a new, aggressive environment, which is harnessing sophisticated tracking technology to squeeze more bangs-per-buck out of ad spend, it sounds a bit weak. Nicky Iapino, general manager of CJ, has summed it up succinctly as follows: 'When I was in radio sales, I used to remember taking a £20,000 budget and I never went back and said this is what you got for your money. I know what these budgets used to be. Online, they almost don't exist. When they spend, people now want to see return, return, return.'

The UK market

In the UK, which of course has traditionally been home to some of the most creative and financially savvy advertising professionals, the online advertising market has grown exponentially over the last few years. It is, however, a brave entrepreneur who decides that he or she will run with a business model which depends on advertising for its prime source of revenues.

Not surprisingly, those who have survived the shakeout and have made money out of online advertising tend to be those businesses which act as middlemen, such as media planning and buying (ilevel.com is a leading, London-based agency) which have guided advertisers to appropriately high-yielding web sites and vice versa.

The main industry body which monitors the UK internet advertising industry is the Internet Advertising Bureau (IAB), headed up by Danny Meadows-Klue, an industry veteran and the former publisher of Electronic Telegraph, the UK's first online version of a daily newspaper. Under his direction, the IAB produces authoritative reports on UK adspend and industry trends.

In its most recent report, published with PriceWaterhouseCoopers in November 2001, the IAB came to the following startling conclusions:

- The total UK internet advertising market in the first half 2001 was £90.2M (GBP63.4M in 2000), showing year on year growth of £26m or 42 per cent.

- Internet advertising was the only advertising sector to show double-digit growth at 42 per cent while most advertising sectors contracted over the same six-month period in 2000.

- Banners continue to represent the largest component of advertising revenue - still generating the most revenues. However, there is real development of additional media formats such as tenancies, nested content, interstitials and sponsorships. All are demonstrating real incremental growth. The trend reflects that of growth in additional formats in the US market.

- By sector, there are significant changes in spending patterns with Automotive, FMCG, Financial Services and Retail relatively strong but entertainment, Media, Technology and Telecoms advertising spend losing share. Again a similar pattern is emerging as was experienced in the US market.

- Internet advertising remains concentrated on top publishers and ad networks, as the largest 10 publishers and ad networks continue to command 89 per cent of total market share.

Source: IAB/PriceWaterhouseCoopers.

What does Meadows-Klue make of these findings? On the subject of why advertisers have moved online, he has said: 'Effective targeting and the unparalleled accountability of online are further reasons why advertisers are continuing to move their spend into the sector. As budgets tighten, online lets them plan with precision accuracy how to deliver and monitor campaigns. The medium has risen to the challenge of tracking return on investment.'

And what does he make of the market as a whole? 'This is real money. Not estimates or conjecture but material cash reported by the finance directors of these companies. Against the words of many commentators, the industry proved it could continue growing year on year.'

Let's take a look at the IAB's figures for UK web sites. These are audited figures, which is a rarity in the internet market. The IAB makes the point, however, that: 'They will give you a benchmark of the relative popularity of different web sites. However, unlike the audits for traditional media, they are not the main currency through which advertisers make their buying decisions as they are counting page traffic rather than reach or frequency. Online campaign planning tends to be based on the more sophisticated tools offered by campaign management systems. Auditing simply provides openness and transparency of data which is what the IAB would like to encourage.'

There are some familiar names in the top 10 most-visited UK web sites, led by Yahoo!, Cricinfo, Rivals and financial site ADVFN and followed by the Guardian newspaper's site, Autotrader, Ireland.com and Liverpool FC. A mighty 67m page impressions from Yahoo! proves the indispensability of its Google-powered search engine and all its various information feeds, but it doesn't necessarily mean it sells much advertising, or at a premium rate. In fact, ADVFN, with half the traffic, will probably sell its banner space at three or four times Yahoo!'s, simply because its users - predominantly ABC1 professionals with high incomes - are more attractive to advertisers than Yahoo!'s indeterminate masses. Nevertheless, although Yahoo! is now branching out into charging for certain parts of its content, it still largely relies on revenues from advertising.

Most UK online businesses are dealing with much more modest traffic figures than these, however. As a general rule of thumb, sites with fewer than 1m page impressions a month will be unattractive to advertisers, unless they are very niche businesses.

Above 1m impressions and the sales houses who specialise in selling bulk inventory will become interested. Or you can try to sell the space yourself. One success story on the latter model is Find.co.uk.

Case Study - Find.co.uk

Find.co.uk was set up in October 1996 - the dawn of time as far as UK internet penetration went - by John Perceval, a former senior executive with Save and Prosper, as a directory of UK financial web sites. The name is an acronym for Financial Information Net Directory. From Day 1, Perceval identified his principal revenue stream as advertising from financial institutions, banks and building societies. He offered them a model they understood and made sure they received monthly data on their adverts' success. Reproduced on page 63 is Find's ratecard, which is published on the web site. It gives a useful insight into the sorts of revenue streams advertising services can generate. As well as straightforward banner ads, Find offers enhanced listings in its directories and so-called 'anchor tenancies', coveted positions which carry a premium. Perceval's web site, which has an enviable reputation in the UK online market, has stuck to a simple but effective business model and continues to thrive thanks to its loyal advertisers and a simple but highly targeted product which consumers return to again and again. At the time of writing, the web site was running no fewer than 74 separate banner campaigns. Simplicity and a thorough knowledge of the financial services industry have been the keys to its success. As the company's web site relates, '[Find] is owned and operated by Omnium Communications Limited which is in turn 100 per cent owned by its three director share holders who have considerable financial services industry marketing experience. Unusual for an internet start up, the company has been profitable for the last four years.'

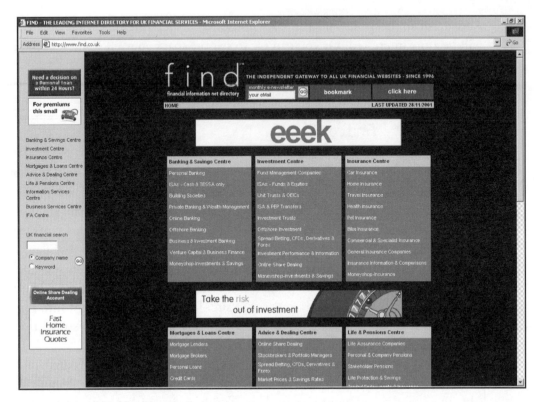

www.find.co.uk

Find.co.uk ratecard

Advertising Rates November 2001
for financial services companies.

Enhanced listings

Enhanced listings give extra prominence and the opportunity to give a description of the client's product or service. It should not exceed 25 words of suitable descriptive copy.

12 months	£600 plus VAT for each promotional listing.
Shorter Periods	£60 plus VAT per month for each promotional listing. Minimum 3 months.

Header listings

One header listing is available at the top of every section. The listing should be one short sentence plus a logo graphic size 80x25.

1 month	£400 plus VAT.

Banner advertisements

Banner advertisements are charged per 1,000 banners served, with no extra charge for appearing on premium sections such as the home page. Banners should not exceed a 15K file size.

Standard banners	468x60 pixels	£30 plus VAT per 1,000 impressions.
Side buttons	120x90 pixels	£20 plus VAT per 1,000 impressions.

Anchor tenancies

Two anchor tenancy slots are available for one month periods, for non-competing products. The tile appears on every page, and for maximum impact all relevant enhanced listings are changed to bold type and placed above the normal alpha order listings.

Anchor tenancy tile	120x60 pixels	£5,000 plus VAT per calendar month.

Find.co.uk ratecard, continued

Monthly E-newsletter

No charge is currently made for suitable articles accepted for inclusion in our monthly E-newsletter, or for the solus position for a tower banner size 125x615. Publication is about 10th of each month; copy date is 4 days before.

Brochure request service

Free of charge for any client with brochures that can be sent out from the client's fulfilment centre, reached by an e-mail request.

Payment-by-results based advertising

Payment-by-results advertising produces quotations, enquiries, policies or subscriptions as relevant - at a known and agreed cost to the client. These arrangements are acceptable if the product is suitable, if the client has reliable tracking systems, and if the client will report results and amounts earned each month. All payments are subject to VAT.

Results reporting

Clients and their authorised agencies can access their logs live on a password protected special Web page. This gives detailed data on banner impressions and click throughs over the chosen time period. They are also sent a full monthly summary, which includes the overall cost per click through.

The future

What does the future hold in store for online advertising models and will people make money out of them? The answers are 'lots' and 'you bet'. If ever there was an aspect of the internet medium that has yet to fulfil its potential, this is it. And particularly in the UK. After the dim, dark days of the mid-90s, when print-based models were recast (with mixed success) by the pioneers such as Electronic Telegraph, Conde Nast and some enlightened advertising agencies, the whole business has been catapulted forward by the advent of accountability, audience-tracking and pay-for-performance. But it is still only the beginning, or rather another beginning. To quote a recent report on internet advertising by BusinessWeek:

'Everything - formats, pricing, measuring, even its purpose - is being rethought - and improved. Yes, this industry has a future.'

What to expect? For a start, clever ads, involving video clips, or so-called 'filmlets': 'chatbots' which enter a dialogue with the surfer, ultimately extracting valuable data from them; and a multitude of viral applications which encourage one user to send ads or special offers on to their friends and family. Think of common promotional gimmicks such as downloadable mini-applications, free wallpaper or screensavers (Guinness, Ford and many other large companies have all had great success with these) and apply 'connectivity' which makes them intelligent - the obvious analogy is perhaps with Excel, which combined the calculator with a word processed document.

Audited web site statistics (calendar month) - leading UK web sites
Source: IAB

Publisher	Site URL	Page Impressions	Users	Audit Period
Yahoo! Europe	www.yahoo.co.uk	676458467	N/A	Jul-01
Cricinfo.com	www.cricinfo.com	254599866	3553168	Mar-01
Rivals Europe Ltd	www.rivals.net	45200513	1090822	Jul-01
Advfn.com Plc	www.advfn.com	36279802	N/A	Mar-01
Guardian Unlimited	www.guardian.co.uk	30949914	N/A	Jul-01
Auto Trader Digital	www.autotrader.co.uk	26572466	964726	Jan-01
Irish Times	www.ireland.com	24658379	1531313	Mar-01
Granada Enterprises (Interactive)	www.liverpoolfc.tv	22569978	1124260	Apr-01
Media Capital Editora multimedia	www.iol.pt	20374017	722971	Feb-01
Associated New Media Limited	www.ukplus.co.uk	14814023	1140468	Jul-01
Situation Publishing	www.theregister.co.uk	15314241	1592329	Mar-01
Ziff-Davis	www.zdnet.co.uk	13537293	1579589	Mar-01
Teletext Ltd.	www.teletext.co.uk	10188667	347971	Jul-01
Moonfruit	www.moonfruit.com	12062892	385517	Mar-01
rightmove.co.uk Ltd	www.rightmove.co.uk	11710944	333878	May-01
Associated New Media Limited	www.thisislondon.co.uk	12391448	706069	Jul-01
GoJobsite	www.gojobsite.co.uk	7580574	N/A	Apr-01
Ziff-Davis	www.gamespot.co.uk	6899887	692239	Mar-01
BMJ Publishing Group	www.bmj.com	5433756	482589	Apr-01

Audited web site statistics (calendar month) - leading UK web sites (continued)   Source: IAB

Publisher	Site URL	Page Impressions	Users	Audit Period
Handbag.com	www.handbag.com	5041864	403282	May-01
Parkers Online	www.parkers.co.uk	4653381	289185	Jan-01
Associated New Media Ltd	www.thisismoney.co.uk	6286472	365990	Jul-01
United Advertising Publications Plc	www.ixm.co.uk	3883446	373856	Jan-01
Associated Newspapers	www.femail.co.uk	3700804	230880	Jul-01
Workthing	www.workthing.com	3513060	289085	May-01
IrishJobs.ie	www.irishjobs.ie	3304903	123983	Jan-01
Prospects	www.prospects.ac.uk	2786805	134854	Jun-01
Chemweb.Inc	www.chemweb.com	1772528	123717	Jun-01
IDG Communications Ltd	www.pcadvisor.co.uk	1070649	80626	Mar-01
BMJ Publishing Group	www.bmjclassified.com	1049383	51370	Apr-01
Top Jobs on the Net Ltd	www.topjobs.ie	788034	62550	Apr-01
Net Resources International Ltd	www.army-technology.com	711910	N/A	Mar-01
Ultimate Communications	www.jobsireland.com	699526	66459	Mar-01

Conclusion

- Although it is currently nigh on impossible to run an online business which is solely dependent on advertising, don't write it off. The ad business is highly cyclical.

- Beware jargon and general advertising bullshit. If in doubt, call the IAB for advice.

- In a downturn, although you may find it difficult to attract advertisers, it is a great time to advertise yourself. Remember that ratecards are simply a starting point - negotiation is all.

Chapter 5

Creating an asset

Chapter 5

Creating an asset

Summary

· Exit strategies: private and public sales
· Online investing
· Conclusion

A business's internet operation, which may encompass much more than simply its web site, is an asset like any other. It may well have its own dedicated staff, its own budgets and its own profit and loss account. It is, therefore, often an asset which may be bought and sold, acquired or divested by a company. Equally, an online business you have set up from scratch has a value, determined by a number of key metrics, mainly focused on its revenue streams and its path to break-even and profitability.

If you are intent on building an online business to groom it for a sale or for a listing on one of the UK stock markets, it is important to take expert advice from the start. Good starting points are simply your accountant and solicitor, not least because the financial and legal structures of any business are the most stringently scrutinised by any prospective purchaser or potential broker or shareholder.

After the recent boom-and-bust cycle, the prospects for online businesses in terms of finding those purchasers or public shareholders remain limited, but by no means non-existent. It is often easier for a company to acquire an existing business (yours, for example) than to build their own from scratch, and this is particularly relevant to online operations, which are costly, time-consuming and prone to nightmarish technical disasters in their earliest set-up phase.

Exit strategies

Private sales

In recent months, many online companies have found homes in larger stables - the acquisition of Smove.com by AssertaHome is just one example. The former was a start-up providing property listings and home-moving advice led by a talented management team with venture capital backing from Eos Ventures (the vehicle established by Jed Simmons, former boss of Excite in the UK). As the online property-listings market matured and consolidated in 2000/2001, it made much sense for a small business such as Smove to join forces with a larger one. Clearly, Smove's management had built an asset (including a large database of editorial content and marketing partnerships) which was valuable to AssertaHome and one which made more sense for them to acquire than to attempt to duplicate from scratch.

The Smove/Assert a Home tie-up was typical of the consolidation which is still taking place in the online property listings market in the UK. The difficulties of aggregating businesses which traditionally were fragmented into hundreds of small estate agency firms have only been overcome by radical changes in the business model used by the bigger online players (such as decisions to drop paid-for listings, for example) and by sheer brute force.

Industry consolidation is, in many ways, not a doom-laden phrase which should summon up images of closure and bankruptcy. To a great extent, it can be music to an entrepreneur's ears. It implies that the particular market segment is maturing and that the larger players are anxious not to get left behind. It is a classic moment for the so-called 'Mom and Pop' businesses to hang a 'For Sale' sign in their window. But that process should really begin at the very start of a business with the 64,000 dollar (and, hopefully, a lot more) question: What is my business's exit? A golden rule for anyone setting up a business to follow is to examine the possible exit opportunities right from the word 'go'. Is your business likely to be attractive to a major player in, say, two years' time? If not, how can you make it so? If yes, should you court that player well in advance, so as to align your business model with one they might be looking for?

The process of selling your business does not have to be a lone quest. There are large numbers of professional teams which exist to buy and sell businesses, to effect introductions and negotiate on companies' behalfs. They do, of course, expect a fee, usually a percentage (typically between five and ten per cent) of the final price that is negotiated. This corporate finance function does, however, release the management of a company from an arduous wade through shark-infested waters. It is often worth investigating hiring a corporate finance advisor at a reasonably early stage in a business, so that you can work with them on 'grooming' a company for sale. Typically these advisors have backgrounds in accountancy and banking and should play a key role in any sale negotiation with some effect.

Public markets

Entrepreneurs who are savvy about making a timely exit from a company they have nurtured will probably prefer a 'trade sale' rather than a listing on the public markets. A trade sale often means a cash deal and although a founding team is often tied in to the new company for a couple of years, in practice these arrangements are frequently renegotiated. An exit onto the public markets is a much more complex one, but can be more lucrative in the long term and is, of course, much more high-profile.

Can an online business still find a home on the London Stock Exchange, or its junior market (Alternative Investment Market)? Undoubtedly, the answer is 'yes', as long as the business meets some important criteria, which are a good deal stricter than they once were. In the heady days of 1999 and early 2000, brokers and investors worried less about revenues, let alone profits, than rather woolly metrics such as growth in web site traffic. Sometimes they simply bought into somewhat spurious - and wildly optimistic - visions about capturing market share and the overturning of traditional businesses. Those days are very much over, but that is not to say that there is no interest in online businesses. Our case study, Ingenta, shows how a solid business model, the prospect of profits and a strong management team can still interest the City.

Furthermore, the City is becoming more comfortable with the online models having been badly burnt by pure dot.com plays which were often flawed for the reasons stated above. Analysts agree on the resilience and the longevity of the internet as a business tool and they understand the business efficiencies it can bring. There are now clear, well-proven examples of revenue-generative businesses which can show a path towards profitability, or increased profitability, and the ability to enhance shareholder value.

The principal reason for a listing, whether it is on the main board of the London Stock Exchange, on AIM or on OFEX (the most junior market and the least regulated) is not, of course, to provide the founders of a business with a short-term exit. It is to raise further capital by the issue of a company's shares to institutions and the public. In practice, however, it often does provide exits, in the medium term, to founders and founder investors. Almost invariably both of these groups are 'locked in' to their shareholdings in the newly public company for at least a year, more often two years, as a show of confidence in their company to the market. There are exceptions - for example, the founders of Lastminute were allowed to sell a small amount of stock at the flotation of the company in March 2000.

The requirements for any public listing are onerous on the company and its directors, and rightly so. As mentioned above, a company must prove it is financially stable and that it satisfies regulatory requirements for its operations. The process of preparing for a flotation is often cited by company directors as the most taxing of their business careers; but the rewards can be substantial and, of course, a public listing does still represent a high point in a company's history. An excellent starting point is to look at the track record of other online businesses which have successfully launched themselves on a public market. These range from the high-profile Lastminute, which used blue-chip investment bank Morgan Stanley to distribute its stock, to small companies such as online auction house icollector, a longtime resident of OFEX, or online cuttings distribution service Clipserver, which moved from OFEX to AIM in late 2000. Because these are public companies they are much more open with their company information and their accounts and prospectuses are easy to find and to study. Also, publicly quoted companies are followed by professional analysts who often make their work available to the general public as well as to their clients.

Case Study - Ingenta

You may not have heard of Ingenta, a British company quoted on AIM, the junior market of the London Stock Exchange, but it is a great online success story, which started life in 1991 as an academic project run by the University of Bath and, at the time of writing, is worth over £90m. Its story is all the more interesting because of the astute financial engineering which has helped build its business.

Ingenta was once Bath Information Data Services - BIDS - which existed to provide online access to research data to students. Some seven years after it was started, the service was spun out of the university and acquired by Mark Rowse, now chief executive of the company, renamed Ingenta. He aggressively expanded the services offered by BIDS and made it the UK's largest online distributor of published research, as he puts it, 'from algebra to zoology.' The vast database which sits behind the web-enabled front end contains links to 2.5m articles from more than 5,200 scientific and academic publications.

How does Ingenta make money? Firstly, the customers can subscribe to the site and then they can receive all the articles for free, or alternatively, they do not have to subscribe but can pay about £15.20 for each article which they download. Equally, publishers are charged fees to have their content on the Ingenta site. Another revenue stream comes from the micro-sites of specialist communities which the company puts together - there are 163 such sites so far, paid for by their 'owners', such as the Organization for Economic Cooperation and Development (OECD). Now, three years after it became a fully commercial operation, Ingenta has 3m unique visitors a month and 10,000 institutional users.

All this activity translates into some chunky numbers. In the six months to 31 March, 2001, the company quadrupled revenues from £1.18m to £4.65m. Although losses widened from £2.17m to £7.27m in the same period, it's hard for analysts and investors to baulk at margins of a whacking 90 per cent. The future looks bright, with analysts expecting pre-exceptional profits of £2.5m by the end of 2002.

Life as a private company is tough enough, but as a quoted one its activites are bound by many more rules and regulations, as well as being answerable to public and institutional shareholders. Nevertheless, Ingenta made its debut on AIM in April 2000 via a reverse takeover of Delyn, an investment vehicle which had £12m in cash. Simply put, the investment vehicle needed a strong, revenue-generative business to justify its existence and Ingenta needed the cash, financial leverage and profile which came with the deal and a quoted entity. At the same time as this reverse takeover there was a placing - a money-raising exercise - of £3m, so Ingenta's cash pile was swelled to £15m. Since its arrival on AIM, the company has seen its share price shoot up to over 250p, plummet to 111p and settle at the time of writing at around 173p, giving it a market capitalisation of £94m.

What are the lessons we can learn from a company such as Ingenta? Firstly, it's clear that Mark Rowse spotted a brilliant application of the internet, with a ready market and, crucially, a low cost base. Sometimes, these sorts of businesses are called 'cash machine businesses' and with reason: once an article is added to the database it will have a shelf life and a revenue potential over a certain period of time. Basically, Ingenta sits back and waits for these two variables to work themselves through. Online picture libraries work on the same model. Clearly, Mr Rowse has researched his market and found tolerable price points for the material he provides access to. You and I may think a £15 charge to download a single article is steep, but the 10,000 institutional clients will be less price-sensitive. In fact, Ingenta's directors will be more interested in attracting large, repeat-paying clients than hundreds of individual customers, which can be expensive to manage. So, the company has identified a solid and loyal customer base, and one which it can sell new products to over time.

Another lesson from Ingenta relates to its progress from academic venture to private company to public company. Clearly it has grown aggressively and marketed itself well to investors and the City. The deal with the investment vehicle Delyn was an astute one, allowing the company to gain cash and a platform from which to, perhaps, make acquisitions of other data companies and increase its share of the burgeoning online data market.

www.ingenta.com

Online investing

Share trading

Five years ago it seemed an unlikely scenario that people would sit at home and trade stocks and shares in real time, supplied with a mass of data and charts which, if not quite putting them on a par with a professional stockbroker, at least levelled the playing field somewhat. This is exactly what has now happened and online trading is now commonplace in the UK. Ask many people how they might make money online and they may well suggest opening an account with Charles Schwab, TD Waterhouse, eTrade or NothingVentured and having a flutter on the FTSE. Clearly, it is not a route for the foolhardy, nor for those who cannot afford to lose their money and all the usual caveats apply, but it is, at least, a new point of access to the stockmarket for investors.

In the beginning, by which I mean around 1996, it was the Americans who introduced us to online trading. Schwab and eTrade became household names in the UK, and the infectious enthusiasm, not to say evangelism, of their mission to educate and enrich the public by allowing them unprecedented access to what was traditionally a stuffy, hidebound industry, was widely reported in the media. Suffice to say, the enthusiasm caught on and in recent years, UK financial institutions have joined the fray. Although online trading is not enjoying the same explosive growth as at one time, the fact is that it has become firmly established, common practice even for small investors among the general public.

The success of online share dealing there encouraged many brokers to set up in the UK and Europe. But let's not get carried away: so far only 4 per cent of UK online consumers have bought shares online, compared with 21 per cent in Germany. Still, although research company Compeer calculated a 42 per cent decline in online trading following the market slump, a look at trading statistics shows the huge growth, starting from a low base, which online trading has enjoyed over the longer term:

UK Internet Share Trading Volumes

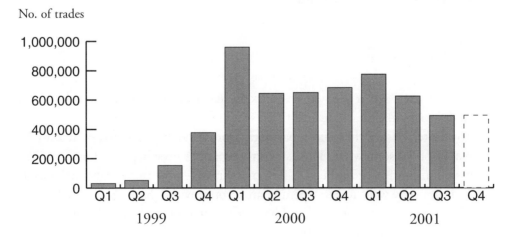

Source: www.compeer.co.uk

Those tempted to join this online band of speculators are strongly advised to follow the old saw: do your own research. There are now many books and regular newspaper columns devoted to online trading, from simple how-to-get-started guides to sophisticated trading strategy compendia. Naturally, there is a mountain of information online, too. One of the best introductions is to be found on Motley Fool, fool.co.uk, which leavens its guidance with good humour and down-to-earth advice.

For the absolute beginner, there is a simple and satisfying way of finding out if you have a talent for online trading: by opening a 'fantasy portfolio' at one of the online brokers and simply following some favourite stocks with an imaginary pot of money and seeing how you do. A good site to try this on is NothingVentured.com, which is run by Durlacher, a London-based stockbroker. Here, for free, you can run an online portfolio and have access to 15-minute delayed share prices, piped in from the London Stock Exchange. For a paid subscription, there are real-time prices, comment and analysis and access to a live trading platform. It is simple to use and an excellent way of deciding if this is for you. Combine this service with a close reading of the *Financial Times*' web site at ft.com and keep half an eye on the bulletin boards of Motley Fool and Interactive Investor, where investors post their (often unreliable) thoughts on stocks they are following and you have yourself a reasonable source of information and data with which to work.

While thousands of people in the UK have dabbled in shares for many years, a practice much popularized by the big privatizations of state-owned companies in the 1980s, there are some for whom it is an all-consuming passion. These so-called 'daytraders', strictly defined as those who open and close their positions in the market during each trading day from 8.30 until 4.30, have decided that they are going to make money solely by trading online. Often they will be in and out of a stock in matter of minutes, responding to share price movements immediately following company announcements, for example. Clearly, these traders thrive best in volatile markets, when there are high volumes of shares traded and large intra-day price changes. It is not for the faint-hearted and for every much-trumpeted gain one day there are often large losses the next.

At one time, when the market was embracing soar-away technology stocks, it seemed as if the UK would follow the example of some Americans and become a nation of daytraders. Indeed, I decided in September 1999 that I would ride this wave, and duly set up a web site called daytrader.co.uk with a modest £5,000 investment. The site simply aggregated share tips from newspapers and brokers' research into a database and provided some daily news. It was a modest success, gaining momentum as the database grew and patterns emerged which, I hope, were of some use to the 10,000-odd subscribers who joined the (free) service. At one point, there was much excitement at an approach from an American company which was intent on opening daytrading centres around the country, but eventually the site was bought by a small broker who wanted a front end to their trading service. It was a fascinating experience, however, watching a mini-phenomenon unfold. Now, daytrader.co.uk is no more and the unbridled enthusiasm of small investors in those heady days has rightly given way to studied caution, but, nevertheless, in its own small way it helped break the mould.

Online trading is still a growth industry and it's true that some people do make a lot of money from it. But it is not necessarily a substitute for the day job. Its growth, and the range of online tools and web sites available to investors, is, to a large extent, dependent on the mood of the stock market. In boom times, there is much activity, often resulting in volatile markets; in bearish ones, volumes can be thin and there are fewer risk-takers. Oh, and do bear in mind: stocks can go down as well as up.

Spread-betting

The internet lends itself perfectly to all manner of gambling and betting, but clearly it is only for the foolhardy or the very brave to venture too far into this often largely unregulated arena. Nevertheless, it is one way of making money online - and of losing it, of course, which is hard to ignore.

There are, of course, reputable and long-established spread-betting houses, which have many thousands of active accounts. The best way to envision the practice of spread-betting is to imagine a stock market exchange crossed with the betting of a racetrack: essentially punters bet on which way a market, or an individual share, is going to move. If they call it right, they win and keep their stake. The market has spread beyond stocks and shares and now encompasses currency prices, futures, options; even sporting events and the unpredictable fortunes of Hollywood stars and the estimated grosses of their latest movies. Spread-betting can be great fun and even lucrative; equally it is most important to understand its vagaries thoroughly before embarking on a first flutter.

One of the best-known spread-betting companies in the UK is IG Index. This company, which is regulated by the Securities and Futures Authority, has been what it calls a 'financial bookmaker' since it was founded in 1974 by Stuart Wheeler. In those days it existed solely to allow UK residents to speculate on the price of gold, however. Having grown considerably since then and now employing over 175 people, the company was floated on the London Stock Exchange in July 2000. On its web site the company points out that, under current UK tax law, all profits are free from UK capital gains and income tax (which normal share dealing is not). This is a key attraction for spread-betters. It also points out that, 'Of course, trading financial markets can result in large losses as well as large profits, and we strongly recommend that you only bet with money you can afford to lose. Although the rewards are potentially unlimited, your maximum possible loss can be capped on most bets using IG's flexible risk management service.'

Other online investments

Although online share dealing and spread-betting seem enticing, even glamorous, let's not forget that there are other investment opportunities online that may not offer day returns (or losses), but are for the longer term. It is well worth checking out building societies, for example, which often offer superior rates of interest on savings deposited in their online accounts. They can afford to do this simply because it is cheaper for them to process online customers than ones who walk off the street. Although some of the fizz has gone out of pure online banks such as Egg, they are also still worth keeping an eye on for special deals aimed at online investors. Mortgages, too, have been through their own internet revolution in the past few years. Many people now apply for mortgages online and may sometimes benefit from reduced arrangement fees and the like. A useful starting point to guide you through the maze of financial services available to internet users is a site such as Thisismoney.co.uk, run by the newspaper group Associated Newspapers, or FTyourmoney.com, the personal finance arm of FT.com.

Case Study - Interactive Investor International

A very early entrant into the financial sector of the internet in the UK, Interactive Investor (iii) is now well known as a personal finance portal and bulletin board resource. Begun in 1995 by entrepreneur Sherry Coutu, the company raised venture capital finance and struck an advertising-for-equity deal with the Telegraph Group to develop its services and attract new users. The company was eventually successfully floated on the Stock Exchange in 1999 by the investment bank Credit Suisse First Boston. Having ridden the rollercoaster of the markets since then, the company was bought by AMP, the Australian finance group, in 2001. How has iii made money over the years? Firstly from advertising - it has traditionally been able to attract premium prices for its banner ad inventory because of the excellent ABC1 demographic profile of its users; secondly, it quickly realised that it could monetise a popular brochure-request service and began charging financial services companies for leads from interested potential customers; and thirdly, while staying away from offering share trading services itself - partly to protect its independent status - iii built trading platforms for a number of other companies. It has been less successful in making money out of its very highly trafficked bulletin boards, which remain free to use, but has diversified into a number of other paid-for services. Users can now access information about ISAs and long-term investments as well as daily share information. Now regarded as one of the long-term survivors of the dot.com boom, iii has an enviable reputation in its market and under its new parent will likely continue to broaden its range of investor services.

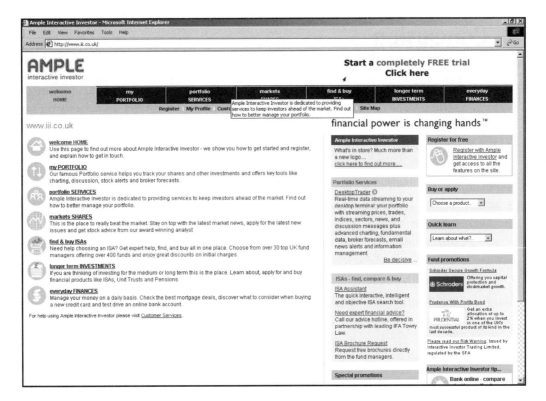

www.iii.co.uk

Conclusion

- Always take professional advice before (a) raising equity; (b) raising debt; (c) selling your business; and (d) acquiring another business. Don't rely on your own instincts. Remember that professional fees can often be negotiated on a success-only basis.

- If you aspire to taking your company to the Stock Market, put the building blocks in place to create a strong management team, a revenue-generative business model and a route to profitability. But also be aware that a listing is often more of a 'beginning' than an 'exit.'

- Although it often seems quicker and slicker on the internet, making money by trading or gambling online is no different to these practices offline. Only use money you can afford to lose.

Index

More books available from Law Pack...

The Legal Guide to Online Business

Going online opens up a world of legal issues that can't be ignored. Domain names, trade marks, international jurisdictions, credit card transactions, partnerships, alliances, online contracts, employee email and internet policies and cyber crimes are some of the issues discussed and explained by specialist solicitor, Susan Singleton. Template documents included.

Code B603	ISBN 1 902646 77 0	PB
250 x 199mm	160pp	£9.99	Nov 2001

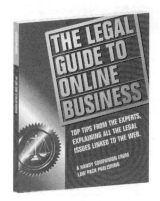

Online Marketing Strategies

What are your goals for your website? Is your website marketing you, or are you marketing it? And how will your website relate to your business's overall marketing strategy? This book provides guidance on building marketing into your website, on monitoring, evaluating and improving your internet or extranet site and on coordinating online and offline marketing strategies.

Code B602	ISBN 1 902646 75 4	PB
250 x 199mm	160pp	£9.99	Oct 2001

Secrets of Successful Websites

Some websites get it right, many get it wrong. This guide divulges what makes a successful site. It covers identifying the audience and their needs, choosing the right model for your site, choosing the right technology and ISP, getting the best help with implementation, design and branding, risk management and testing procedures.

Code B601	ISBN 1 902646 74 6	PB
250 x 199mm	160pp	£9.99	Nov 2001

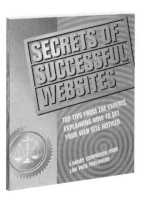

To order, visit www.lawpack.co.uk or call 020 7940 7000

More books available from Law Pack...

Limited Company Formation

Incorporation as a limited liability company is the preferred structure for thousands of successful businesses. *Limited Company Formation Made Easy* Guide explains why, and shows you how to set up your own limited liability company easily and inexpensively. It provides detailed but easy to follow instructions, background information, completed examples of Companies House forms and drafts of other necessary documents.

Code B503	ISBN 1 902646 43 6	PB
250 x 199mm	112pp	£9.99	1st edition

Profitable Mail-Order

Mail-order business is big business, and it's growing year by year. Setting up and running your own mail-order business can be fun as well as profitable. This *Made Easy* Guide shows you how to do it, explaining the vital importance of product profile, building valuable mailing lists, effective advertising and a whole lot more. It divulges the mail-order secrets that ensure success!

Code B510	ISBN 1 902646 46 0	PB
250 x 199mm	206pp	£9.99	1st edition

Running Your Own Business

You have a business idea that you want to put into action, but you also want advice on the realities of setting up and running a business: this *Made Easy* Guide is for you. It takes you through the business-creation process, from assessing your aptitude and ideas, to funding and business plans.

Code B511	ISBN 1 902646 47 9	PB
250 x 199mm	140pp	£9.99	1st edition

To order, visit www.lawpack.co.uk or call 020 7940 7000